THE ROCKEFELLER FAMILY GARDENS

An American Legacy

THE ROCKEFELLER FAMILY GARDENS

An American Legacy

PHOTOGRAPHS BY LARRY LEDERMAN

Introduction by Dominique Browning

Essays by Cynthia Bronson Altman
Todd Forrest and Cassie Banning

Afterword by Larry Lederman

THE MONACELLI PRESS

Pages 2–3: View from the West Terrace at Kykuit to the Hudson River with Marino Marini's Horse *(left) and Aristide Maillol's* Night *installed on the lawn.*

Pages 4–5: A display of early fall color on a thread leaf maple tree near the entrance to the Japanese Garden at Kykuit.

Pages 6–7: Spirit Path at the Abby Aldrich Rockefeller Garden in Seal Harbor, Maine.

Page 8: Moon Gate at the Abby Aldrich Rockefeller Garden.

First published in the United States by The Monacelli Press

Library of Congress Control Number 2016956441
ISBN 978-158093-487-9

Design by Susan Evans, Design per se

The Monacelli Press
236 West 27th Street
New York, New York 10001

Printed in Singapore

THE ROCKEFELLER FAMILY GARDENS

Dominique Browning

Most of us think of water as being essential to gardens; it is perhaps the first association that comes to mind. Keeping a garden properly watered. Bringing water into the garden for boggy plantings. Watching the play of a breeze across the water of a reflecting pool. Or filling a vase, so that the flowers of our labor can linger indoors with us just a bit longer.

The photographer, however, considers something else to be fundamental to the life of a garden. He watches the light. The light that throws lines into relief, the light that sets maple leaves ablaze, the light that slicks stone with a glistening sheen, the gloaming light that picks out the white blossoms so that they linger, like ghosts, as the day dies. And then there is the breathtaking experience of an early light catching the trunk of a tree or an afternoon light dazzling us with color. These are the moments of light that etch images vividly into our memories.

These are the impressions captured by photographer Larry Lederman in this new book. What you are holding is a marriage of some of the most ephemeral of our arts. Gardens are like the mandalas of the Buddhists. Just as the monks slowly lay down their colored chalks, so do gardeners painstakingly design, plant, and tend seed and soil. The fierce winds of time might blow away years of effort. Even if fortune is gentle, and a gardener is there to lovingly tend a place for generations, a garden will change with the rebirth of every spring. Nothing remains the same.

It is the photographer who is able to seize such fleeting enchantment, who fixes this endless cycle of light, of beauty, of imagination. It is fitting that Lederman's description of his first visit to Kykuit should be of the gleam of leaves and trunks and bright red sculpture in a heavy rain. Click. The garden, strong and handsome as it is, immediately commanded his attention. He returned with his camera for many years, to see what he could see. And to think about what we should see.

Lederman and his camera also visited the Abby Aldrich Rockefeller Garden on Mount Desert in Maine. Rain, fog, mist, and ocean: all these work on the unique light of Maine, and for Lederman, heightened the mystical feeling of the garden's Spirit Path. These visits have given us, as readers, the rare privilege of being able to contemplate, in some depth, two of the country's most important gardens.

The Maine garden is a precious part of American history. It was designed by Beatrix Farrand, a founding member of the American Society of Landscape Architects in 1899—and its only woman founder. The niece of Edith Wharton (who was a lifelong friend of Henry James, which should tell you all you need to know about the milieu in which she worked), Farrand designed gardens for the White House, for Princeton University, for Yale University. Very little of her work survives; a beautiful example is Dumbarton Oaks, in Washington, D.C. Another is the Rockefeller garden in Maine, a blend of Asian and European styles, on land carved out of an old forest. While she was working on it in the late 1920s, Farrand commuted from her home in California to Maine by train.

In Maine, Lederman set up his camera at various points, in various lights, in the Oval Garden, along the Spirit Path, at the Moon Gate. He pays homage to the seated Buddha Shakyamuni, a seventeenth-century gilt-bronze piece. In New York, at Kykuit, Lederman is clearly entranced with the rich colors not only of perennial beds, but also of spring and autumn leafing. He captures, too, the whimsy and thoughtfulness of the placement of sculpture among the trees and in garden rooms.

Kykuit is the Dutch word for "lookout"; the house is situated high above the Hudson River. The grounds were originally laid out by Olmsted Brothers, sons of Frederick Law Olmsted, who designed Manhattan's Central Park. You can see the Olmsted influence in the gentle curves of the drives through pastoral sections of the estate, passing some magnificent trees. John D. Rockefeller was an exigent client and had a hand in all of the planning. (And, to close out a too-brief social history of the golden age of American estates, the interiors of the mansion were furnished by Ogden Codman Jr.—who teamed up with Edith Wharton in 1897 to write *The Decoration of Houses*, a foundational text in American interior design.)

In 1906, Rockefeller hired architect William Welles Bosworth to organize vistas and design terraces, fountains, temples, and pavilions. The Kykuit gardens are considered the finest examples of his Beaux-Arts style in the United States.

Most garden books are illustrated with compilations of photographs, and sometimes those views are not necessarily compatible. That, of course, can be useful. But it is a completely different experience, and a deeply moving one, to visit gardens through the eyes of one artist—especially when those gardens themselves have been in the devoted care of generations of one family.

Lederman is lucky enough to live near Kykuit, so he could return whenever the mood (his, or the garden's) struck him. No other book or article has so thoroughly covered these gardens—indeed, this is the first time extensive images of the Japanese Garden at Kykuit have been published. Lederman is, by vocation, a lawyer. As a photographer, he is self-taught; he picked up a camera fifteen years ago, deciding he could learn a great deal about handling light by studying the work of landscape painters.

In conversation, Lederman describes his process as a "playing with the light," especially in the Japanese gardens; he is "moving the sun," he says, as he moves his camera around the elements in his compositions. He learned to do this during what he calls a "life-changing" project, which was to photograph the trees on the grounds of the New York Botanical Garden.

Lederman teases out the singularities of the Rockefeller gardens, highlighting the way garden rooms are composed, views framed, plantings distributed. He has an intimacy with these gardens that can only come over years of close attention. These photographs are his memories, but they become ours, as well, as if we had visited in a dream.

To enter so richly into another person's vision is a form of collaboration. We give ourselves over to the photographer's gift, and in so doing, our way of seeing is also altered, refined. A photograph is much more than a click of the shutter. It is an act of composition and editing, and there are dozens of decisions to be made— sometimes in the blink of an eye. Where is the frame? What ought to be central? Where is the light? What foreshadows the approach of a new season? Where is the trace of a season coming to a close?

We can only hope that these gardens will enjoy many more seasons, that they will give visitors yet another century of pleasure. But with Lederman's photographs, we have a record of this treasure for all time. Once you have wandered through these photographs, you will look out over your landscapes with new eyes. What any art, however ephemeral, does best is to alter our consciousness. Gardens may vanish, but if we are lucky, they can leave a lasting impression.

The Formal Gardens at Kykuit

CYNTHIA BRONSON ALTMAN

High above the Hudson River near Tarrytown, New York, John D. Rockefeller established a country retreat as an escape from the bustling life in Manhattan, the family's primary place of business and residence. The house was called Kykuit, based on the Dutch word for "lookout," which the early settlers had given to the hill. Today the property is a site of the National Trust for Historic Preservation, under the stewardship of the Rockefeller Brothers Fund, and is a center for its philanthropic activities.

Rockefeller searched for land in an area that he had come to know through visiting his younger brother William, who had renovated Rockwood Hall, a property with lavish gardens on the banks of the Hudson River a few miles north of Tarrytown.

Rockefeller and his son, John D. Rockefeller Jr., assembled a number of parcels to create an estate of more than three thousand acres.[1] Over the course of a century, a number of distinguished landscape architects have shaped the 250-acre grounds within the gates, and the landscape has matured and evolved to reflect the layered visions of the three generations of the Rockefeller family to live there.

John D. Rockefeller valued broad expanses of fields and lawns, groves of beeches, horse chestnuts, and birches in the distances, and at the far perimeters a noble forest of evergreens—spruce, hemlock, pines, and cedar, which defined the boundaries in winter. His son focused on ordering the landscape in a more formal Beaux-Arts garden design, with strong axes and clearly defined garden rooms. For Nelson Rockefeller, these garden rooms and terraces provided the setting for an extensive collection of twentieth-century sculpture, which is still in place today.

JOHN D. ROCKEFELLER

Rockefeller had retired from active leadership of Standard Oil on 1896, but not formally until a number of years later. Pocantico became an important place of retreat from the rigors of life in Manhattan.[2] His vision was one of the redemptive power of landscape, as embodied by the eighteenth-century English tradition and by Frederick Law Olmsted's natural landscapes of the late nineteenth and early twentieth centuries in America. To this Rockefeller added the veneration of open vistas, grand expanses to a vast wilderness—an ideal, a view of boundless nature—the vocabulary of national identity defined by the western frontier. Admiring the firm's designs for Rockwood Hall, John D. Rockefeller called on Olmsted, Olmsted & Eliot to begin the process of executing his vision for Kykuit. The archive at the Olmsted National Historic Site in Brookline, Massachusetts, preserves more than fifty maps and plans from 1895 and 1896, with labels including "Temporary grading at top of Kaakout Hill," "Preliminary Study for House Site," and "Approach Drives and other Arrangements Near House," date from the time that Warren Manning, then on their staff, spent a number of months at Pocantico. Additional documents from

Top: Terrace and rill leading to the teahouse in the Inner Garden as designed by William Welles Bosworth.

Above: Sheep grazing on the lawn.

Opposite: Kykuit site plan.

Preceding pages: The proportions and plantings of the forecourt elegantly complement the stature of the house.

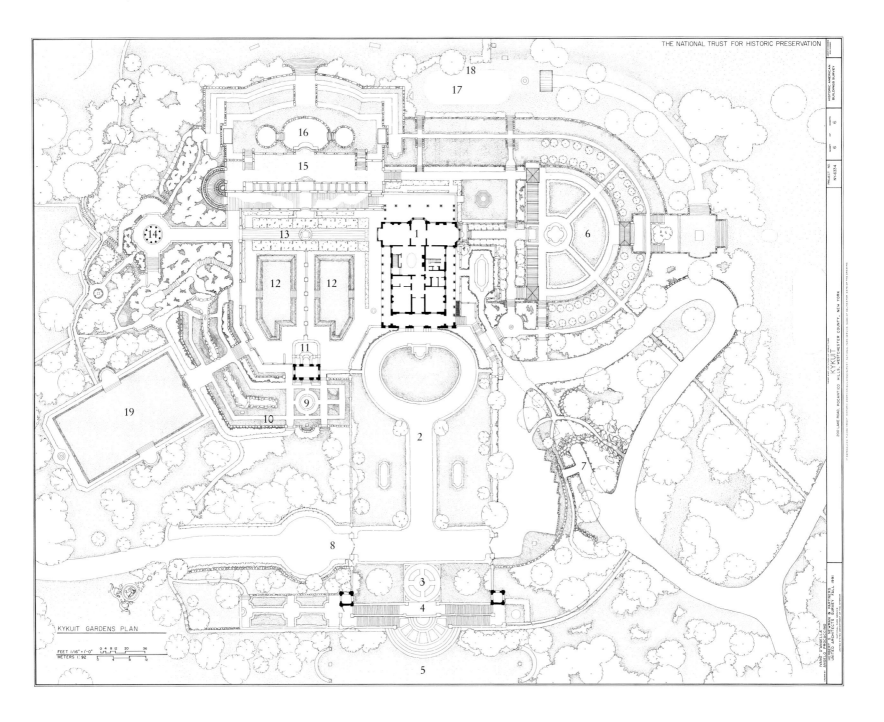

KYKUIT GARDENS PLAN

FEET 1/16" = 1'-0" 0 4 8 12   20   36
METERS 1:192

1. Kykuit
2. Forecourt
3. Oceanus fountain
4. Grand staircase

5. Eastern Terrace
6. Rose Garden
7. 1909 gate
8. 1913 gate

9. Morning Garden
10. Brook Garden
11. Teahouse
12. Inner Garden

13. Linden Allée
14. Temple
15. Orange Tree Terrace
16. Swimming Pool
    Terrace

17. Putting green
18. Entrance to Japanese
    Garden
19. Tennis lawn

the late 1920s and early 1930s detail plantings for the lower terraces and some of the smaller gardens.[3]

Perhaps the greatest of the Olmsted contributions (a concept also claimed by JDR) was the road that carves into the hill, where at each turn the views gradually unfold, finally reaching a crescendo at the summit, revealing the majesty of the Hudson River, the cliffs of the Palisades, and the mountains beyond.

Rockefeller took great pleasure in the work of planning, particularly laying out roads, which he described as "my special hobby." As he wrote in his brief memoir, *Random Reminiscences of Men and Events*:

> I thought I had the advantage of knowing every foot of the land, all the old big trees were personal friends of mine, and with the views at any given point I was perfectly familiar . . . How many miles of roads I have laid out in my time, I can hardly compute . . . While surveying roads, I have run the lines until darkness made it impossible to see the little stakes and flags.[4]

The groves of maple and copper beeches, the elms in the forecourt and on the terraces were all relocated as mature trees, and Rockefeller relished his success in this challenge:

> In nursery stock, as in other things, the advantage of doing things on a large scale reveals itself. The pleasure and satisfaction of saving and moving large trees—trees, say from ten to twenty inches in diameter, or even more in some cases, has been for years a source of great, interest . . . We have moved trees ninety feet high, and many seventy or eighty feet. And they naturally are by no means young. At one time or another we have tried almost all kinds of trees, including some which the authorities said could not be moved with success.[5]

Rockefeller took up golf as a form of exercise in the late nineteenth century, and the game quickly became a favorite pastime. He set up four holes at Kykuit in 1899, and in 1901 acquired a country club in Lakewood, New Jersey, which he renamed "Golf House." In 1902 he commissioned the design

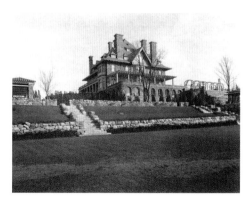

Top: West facade in 1908 before the house was rebuilt.

Above: Pool in the Morning Garden. The arabesques of clipped box were designed by Olmsted Brothers in 1934.

Top: Inner Garden, with fancifully clipped box from Holland, c. 1909.

Above: The Rockefeller bookplate with an engraving of the Temple of Aphrodite, based on a rendering by William Welles Bosworth.

of the Pocantico golf course from Willie Dunn Jr., renowned golfer and designer, who also worked at the courses at Apawamis in Rye, New York, and Shinnecock Hills in Southampton, the oldest in the country. Rockefeller played daily, and Pocantico was his favorite, by far, of the courses on his various properties.

A 1919 article in *International Studio* reported in addition to golf, the gardens gave him great pleasure:

> But those who have had the good fortune to see the beauties of Pocantico Hills . . . with Mr. Rockefeller himself as a guide, will tell you that his greatest enthusiasm now seems to be centered in the wonderful gardens which he has caused to be created there.[6]

JOHN D. ROCKEFELLER JR.

Between 1906 and 1913, John D. Rockefeller Jr. oversaw the design and completion of Kykuit and its gardens for his father.[7] The Beaux-Arts gardens immediately surrounding the house were the vision of architect William Welles Bosworth and were substantially complete by 1908. Trained at MIT and the École des Beaux-Arts in Paris, Bosworth also worked in London as an assistant to artist Sir Lawrence Alma-Tadema, renowned for his historical paintings set in ancient Rome and Greece. Bosworth's architectural designs referenced the classical world, using a vocabulary reinforced by his experiences in London and his studies in Paris.

In the late nineteenth century, the vocabulary of Italian gardens was considered the epitome of beauty in garden design. Both the Rockefellers and Bosworth would have been familiar with the many publications in circulation. Among them was Charles A. Platt's 1894 *Italian Gardens,* nineteen essays that documented Renaissance and Baroque gardens with plans and more than one hundred photographs.[8] A decade later, *Italian Villas and Their Gardens* by Edith Wharton with twenty-six watercolor illustrations by Maxfield Parrish became a touchstone in the study, detailing more than seventy-five villa gardens. Bosworth echoed the unique elements of these designs and often quoted quite literally from specific gardens with his use of grottos, terraces, and grand staircases.

Kykuit's gardens include replicas of fountains from the Boboli Gardens and the Pitti Palace, a pair of large candelabra of veined stone from Hadrian's Villa, a classical temple and sculpture of the Medici Venus, and a structure echoing a pavilion at the Villa Lante. While Italian influences were predominant, French design is evident in the allées of pleached linden and maple, and Islamic tradition in the rill studded with gentle jets of water, a feature of the gardens of the Alhambra in Spain.

To imbue the gardens with the patina of age, Bosworth brought wellheads from Venice and purchased ancient Etruscan oil jars, columns, and fountains from the auction of the estate of Stanford White in November 1907. Carved marble sarcophagi, busts of Roman senators, and marble versions of the Borghese and Warwick vases—famed archeological discoveries—grace the gardens and pergolas.[9]

In an article in the *American Architect* in 1911, Bosworth outlined the tenets of his design philosophy, all evident in the Kykuit gardens:

> We think that to give it such a character it should contain water, the very life of a garden; variety, so achieved as not to disturb the feeling that each feature is a part of the whole and linked together with it. Shade, as well as sunshine; sequestered and obscure places, tempting one to explore them, as well as open exposures; points especially adapted from which to enjoy the best views; and places screened and sheltered, where one may get away from the view. Places to keep cool in, and places to sun oneself in; places to walk and places to sit; bird notes and running water for sounds, and the flowers and fruit trees for color, odor, and taste; in fact all the senses should be appealed to in the ideal garden. And one must not forget the note of antiquity.[10]

The steep slope of the site lent itself to terracing, both to the east and the west. The plan is defined by garden rooms to the south of the house and two strong

Top: Maxfield Parrish, Boboli, *illustration for Edith Wharton's seminal study* Italian Villas and Their Gardens.

Above: Postcard of the Brook Garden, here referred to as the Morning Garden.

Top: Rose Garden with an evergreen maze in the north quadrant (removed in 1915).

Above: Italian Garden in the early 1970s.

axes, east–west from the forecourt through the house to the river vista and north–south from the classical temple through the primary rooms of the house to the Rose Garden or Circular Garden on the north. The Inner Garden or Walled Garden on the south side of the house was the formal garden, with parallel sunken lawn bordered by box. Beyond is the Brook Garden, where perennials and weeping cherries line the banks of a meandering stream. The adjacent Morning Garden to the south and east of the house, catches the early sun and holds the spring warmth.

During the time that John D. Rockefeller Jr. was working with Bosworth, he and his family lived down the hill in a large rambling house called Abeyton Lodge. They moved to Kykuit after his father's death in 1937. While a simplification of the forecourt and some changes to the gardens were discussed, most were not carried out, and the gardens remained largely unchanged during their residence.

NELSON A. ROCKEFELLER

The children of John D. Rockefeller Jr. and Abby Aldrich Rockefeller grew up knowing well the gently rolling hills and lawns, the stepped terraces, and garden rooms at Kykuit. When JDR Jr. died in 1960, the house and gardens were inherited jointly by the next generation, and Nelson, the second son, took on its care and maintenance.

Nelson Rockefeller brought to the gardens a superb collection of twentieth-century sculpture, installing nearly eighty works by European and American masters, including Picasso, Maillol, Moore, Arp, Marini, Calder, Nadelman, Nevelson, Lachaise, and David Smith within the fieldstone walls, on the terraces, and across the lawns of the golf course. In some of the gardens, plantings were modified to accommodate the sculpture. For example, box topiaries were simplified to conical forms to bring focus to the figurative forms, and the floral displays became less elaborate.

Rockefeller took great pleasure in identifying the perfect setting for each piece:

I am particularly interested by the problem of relating art to architecture, as it was related in the past. Hanging pictures, finding new spatial relationships for my sculpture . . . this is my own way of being creative . . . I seriously considered being an architect when I was in college; perhaps my love for sculpture is related to my forgotten vocation.[11]

In the russet groves of copper beeches, carpeted with the deep green pachysandra, he placed the vibrant orange *Above II* by Alexander Liberman and the gleaming white fiberglass *Granny's Knot* by Shinkichi Tajiri. He was keenly aware of the power of form in the landscape, reserving the far edges of the sweeping lawns for the monumental sculptures by Clement Meadmore and Tony Smith.

Describing his role in "arranging the art of others in nice settings and beautiful places," Rockefeller said:

I happen to be one of those who feel that the joining of the creations of the beauty of nature with the creations of individuals whether it be architecture, landscape gardening or sculpture or whatnot, that they both enhance each other. And this to me is something that is very meaningful, because, not being able to create things, the only thing that I can do is to try to arrange them . . . [for] the enjoyment of the piece, whatever it happens to be—painting, sculpture—but the piece in the right setting or in the right combination.[12]

Nelson Rockefeller altered some of the gardens. In the early 1960s, he brought David Engel to the Japanese Garden to expand the original hill and pond garden, adding a meditation garden of raked sand and groves of maple and bamboo. In the early 1970s, the landscape architect Marquis GB Guerrieri Gonzaga from Rome created a new design for the Italian Garden below the *Oceanus* and suggested changes to the Rose Garden.

Above: Allée in the Italian Garden, photographed by Mattie Edwards Hewitt, 1929.

Opposite: Alexander Liberman's Above II *was installed in the copper beech grove by Nelson Rockefeller. Here the tree trunks and sculpture glisten after an afternoon rain.*

TOUR OF THE GARDENS

The monumental fountain *Oceanus and the Three Rivers*, a replica of Giambologna's work of 1570–74, commands the forecourt. From there the axis extends through the house to the Hudson and the Palisades on the far shore. Maxfield Parrish's painting of this fountain in the Boboli Gardens graced the cover of many editions of Edith Wharton's *Italian Villas and Their Gardens*. The Kykuit fountain also links the rivers of the new world to the old; in the late nineteenth and early twentieth centuries, the beauty and majesty of the Hudson was often compared to that of the Rhine.

The sculptor Raffaello Romanelli carved this version in Carrara marble in Florence.[13] The figures were shipped in fourteen crates, arriving on the steamer *Berlin* on May 27, 1914, and assembled on site. Oceanus towers above personifications of the three rivers of the ancient world, the Nile, the Ganges, and the Euphrates. Each holds a ewer that pours water into the massive granite bowl below. Quarried on Crotch Island near Stonington, Maine, the bowl was shipped on the three-masted schooner *Susan N. Pickering*, also arriving on the banks of the Hudson in May 1914.

Between the fountain and the house, six towering elms once shaded the forecourt. These were transplanted to the site as mature trees, which must have pleased JDR. They succumbed to Dutch elm disease, and were replaced in the early 1980s by honey locust, chosen to echo the shape of the elms.

THE INNER GARDEN

The Inner Garden, Inclosed (historic spelling) Garden, or Walled Garden is off the south porch of the house. Today, as in Bosworth's design, two sunken lawns are bordered by low hedges of ilex (once box), and conical yews mark the corners. Bosworth described the planting material:

> The topiary boxwood . . . was brought from Holland and the ancient myrtle trees in boxes by the Tea House pool came from an old French villa.

Opposite: The entry drive passes through wrought-iron gates supported by massive stone piers to arrive in the forecourt, where the Oceanus fountain is on axis with the entrance to the house.

The color scheme of the flower borders in this garden in yellow and white, dwarf pansies and snapdragons alternating spring and fall.[14]

Early photographs illustrate the exuberance of this garden with ornamental box in fancifully clipped forms, myrtle, bay, and oleander in pots, and orange trees in wooden boxes, *caisses de Versailles*, modeled on those at the French royal palace. Other period photographs illustrate a great density and variety of the plantings on the south porch. Today the space has been simplified and rectangular gray wooden boxes are planted with annuals each year.

The teahouse of rough-cut fieldstone is similar in proportion and design to a pavilion at the sixteenth-century Villa Lante, photographed by Charles A. Platt and published in his *Italian Gardens*.[15] In front of the teahouse water cascades in a tiered fountain from a large scallop shell into four graduated pools, each with fanciful gilt-bronze fountain spouts of alligators, sea horses, snails, crabs, and frogs by François Michel Louis Tonetti.

Throughout the gardens and fountains, Bosworth installed an elaborate lighting system similar to that at the Pan-American Exposition in Buffalo in 1901, where he had been the on-site architect for Carrère & Hastings. Bosworth described the overall effect:

> A canal links the fountain of the Tea House with a Moorish-shaped basin lined with bronze . . . the line of the canal is broken from place to place by basins and water-jets which are lighted from beneath. Seen from the house terrace, they produce an effect resembling that of a jeweled necklace, the bronze basin framing the pendant. Practically all of the fountains and grottos are illuminated at night by concealed lights within them . . . [T]he reflection of the polished brass, lifted up by the water, gives a keynote of color to this part of the garden, all the flowers being white and golden yellow.[16]

Opposite: The Inner Garden is below the south porch. Conical evergreens and twentieth-century sculpture punctuate the broad lawns and bluestone terrace. To the east is the teahouse designed by Bosworth.

THE ALLÉE TO THE TEMPLE

The north–south axis of the plan is formed by the Linden Allée between the
house and between a classical temple designed by Bosworth, with the sculpture
of Aphrodite, or the Medici Venus. When this figure first came to the gardens in
1915, Bosworth supported the attribution to the fourth-century B.C.E. Athenian
sculptor Praxiteles. Today experts accept the sculpture as an eighteenth- or nineteenth-century replica of the Medici Venus in the Uffizi, an image that graces
many European and American gardens.[17] The twenty-two European linden,
which are pruned twice a year, date to 1908. The path to the temple is now bordered by white astilbe, where peonies and potted hydrangea were used earlier.
This axis continues into the house, through the library, alcove (or tearoom), and
dining room to the Rose Garden.

*Opposite and above: The
Linden Allée extends from
the house to the Temple of
Aphrodite.*

Above: Grotto in the Brook Garden.

Opposite: Streams and paths meander through the Morning Garden. In the adjacent Brook Garden is a cipollino marble column surmounted by a sphere and a figure of Winged Victory.

THE BROOK GARDEN

Double gates at the south end of the Inner Garden lead to a garden where weeping cherries border a brook that flows from a dark and cavernous grotto. Nearly two tons of cave material were brought in to impart rusticity to the walls and grottos: "Water drips from stalactites in the roof, which were imported from Genoa for this purpose, and falls on an ancient bronze Chinese water drum, filling the air with low toned-music."[18]

According to Bosworth:

> The crowning glory of the Kijkuit gardens is seen when the Rock Garden is in its fullest bloom. The margins of the brook are planted profusely with every variety of iris overshadowed with dwarf flowering fruit trees and pink and white dogwood against a background of white lilacs and cedar trees. Thus the color scheme ranges from white to pink and lavender and palest yellow.[19]

In the 1930s, much of John D. Rockefeller Jr.'s attention was absorbed by the restoration of Colonial Williamsburg, where he came to know the work of Arthur A. Shurcliff. In 1936 Shurcliff was asked to present a plan to revitalize some of the gardens at Kykuit. His planting plan for the Brook Garden lists nearly sixty perennials and bulbs, including clematis and columbine, larkspur, lobelia, lady's slipper, wild sweet William, trillium, many varieties of lilies and violets, speedwell, and yarrow.[20] During Nelson Rockefeller's residency, the plantings were simplified, and the dense green of hosta, ferns, and ivy encouraged a focus on the modern sculpture. Today the garden has once again become a profusion of color with perennials that reflect the Shurcliff plan.

THE MORNING GARDEN

The Morning Garden, just behind the teahouse, catches the sun early in the day, and even in winter the laurels and rhododendron provide an evergreen haven. A shallow circular pool of pink marble served as a wading pool for the young children. In the center is a gilt-bronze fountain spout of a playful putto riding a sea monster by Tonetti. The four quadrants around the pool were once arabesques of closely clipped box, designed by the Olmsted firm in 1934. A bronze Winged Victory towers seventeen feet above the pool on a column of cipollino marble with Corinthian capital acquired at the auction of the estate of Stanford White in 1907.

THE TERRACES

"The general form of the hill was that of any oyster shell, flat only at the top, and hardly flat there," wrote Bosworth, explaining the challenge of the site, which he resolved with terraces that descend from the house and upper gardens to the west toward the Hudson.[21] The densely planted hills in the distance suggest that the property extends to the banks of the river and obscure the village neighborhoods and railroad in between. The grand staircase leads down to the Orange Tree Terrace, once shaded by as many as twenty-six large orange trees in wooden planters, *cassis de Versailles*; these trees were moved seasonally to and from winter storage in the nearby Orangerie. The terrace is edged by a railing of intricately intertwined grape vines designed by Tiffany. *The Goose Girl,* a bronze figure by Karl Bitter commissioned for the gardens in 1914, stands in a shallow niche lined with stalactite material imported from Genoa.

Three pools, used as swimming pools, center the next terrace. Concentric circles of black and white pebbles mimic the ripples of the water; rough-hewn steps of natural stone descend into the central pool, which is fed by water from a stalactite-lined grotto. Stone bridges lead to the smaller pools, each with a sixteenth-century sculpture of a triton holding a trumpet. Tubs of jasmine once stood before the pavilions at either end of the terrace. The broad flight of stone steps to the lowest terrace is flanked by two monumental sculptures, *Hercules and the Hydra* and *Hercules and the Nemean Lion*, attributed to Orazio Marinali.

Above: Rose garden photographed by Mattie Edwards Hewitt, 1929.

Opposite: The terraces overlooking the Hudson include swimming pools and a whimsical pergola furnished with a mushroom-shaped cast-stone table and stools.

THE ROSE GARDEN

The north–south axis terminates in the Rose Garden or Circular Garden, one of Abby Aldrich Rockefeller's favorite spaces. When first designed, an evergreen maze filled the northern quadrant; this was removed in 1915 and replaced with roses. Correspondence refers to standard white roses from England over five feet high, Mme Plantier and Wichuriana, and Yellow Persian, and gardenia roses (a soft creamy yellow) and Lady Gay roses, a light pink rambler.[22]

In addition to the roses, the historical plantings were more elaborate with borders of hollyhocks and peonies, daisies and heliotrope, and the rarer varieties of decorative plantings, and blossoming fruit trees. A lattice trellis, with privet on one side and hawthorn on the other, once bordered the circular space. A double row of columnar juniper was planted in the 1970s, but this, too, was removed.

Today a pergola, once wisteria covered, stands along the southern side. In the center is a three-tiered fountain with a marble Boy and Goose, a facsimile of a one now in the Pitti Palace in Florence, and once at the Medici Villa at Castello.[23] The plantings are ever-changing with polyantha, Katarina Zymat, 'China Doll' and 'the Fairy', and such hybrid teas as Mr. Lincoln, Tiffany, Queen Elizabeth, and Peggy Rockefeller as well as some of the original choices.

THE ITALIAN GARDEN

When first designed by Bosworth, this *giardino segreto* (small private garden) on a landing of the stair below the Oceanus, contained an allée of London planetrees and a carpet of English ivy bordering a path to a marble replica of the Vatican *Sleeping Ariadne*.[24] The design was intact in 1929, and was documented in the series of photographs of the gardens by Mattie Edwards Hewitt. Gradually the surrounding trees shaded the space and the planetrees were replaced by dogwood, more apt to thrive in dappled sun. In the early 1970s, an entirely new design was commissioned by Nelson Rockefeller from the Marquis GB Guerrieri Gonzaga of Rome. He created a formal architectonic space with four boxwood *parterres de broderie*, arabesques designed to be seen from above. While a departure from

Opposite: The focal point of the Rose Garden is the Boy and Goose fountain. The semicircular space is enclosed by a boxwood hedge punctuated with pavilions.

Bosworth's original design, the scrolled forms echoed those used in the Morning Garden and near the Rose Garden, both designs no longer extant by the 1960s. Today again a "secret garden," the space awaits restoration.

THE PALM HOUSE, CUTTING GARDEN, AND ORANGERIE

To the north, down-hill from the house and below the Coach Barn, the land levels out to the north gate. This was the site of several auxiliary structures supporting the extensive gardens, including greenhouses, a Palm House or conservatory, and an Orangerie.

In 1906 the well-known firm of Lord & Burnham was contracted to build a glass-domed palm house for propagation and for overwintering the palms, bay, oleander, and other tropical plants placed throughout the gardens. Plans for it can be found in the archives of the New York Botanical Garden. The structure was dismantled in the early 1930s at a time of simplification throughout the estate, but the green-houses from that time remain.

The level area near the Palm House was the site of a cutting garden designed by Beatrix Jones Farrand in 1906. The plan preserved in her papers, now at the University of California, Berkeley, documents the suggested plantings (79 were listed) and a period photograph illustrates its form.

In March 1908, Bosworth was asked to design a "tree storage house at Pocantico" to accommodate "an unrivaled collection of dwarf orange trees" said to be more than two hundred years old. They were bought at auction from the collection of the Marquis d'Aux at a chateau near Le Mans.[25] The shipment arrived in May and protection from the harsh winters of the northeast was needed. In overall design and proportion, Bosworth drew on the Orangerie at Versailles. On the west facade are ten tall arched windows to admit as much sunlight as possible. The interior walls are painted white to reflect and thus increase the winter light from windows and skylights. Thick masonry walls absorb and hold the heat provided by the boilers so that an interior temperature of just above freezing could be maintained.

Top and above: The Orangerie, which sheltered a collection of dwarf orange trees in winter.

The bay and orange trees were deaccessioned twice. In 1935, as several areas of operation on the estate were being simplified, John D. Rockefeller Jr. donated them to several botanic gardens. In the 1960s, Nelson Rockefeller worked with Bosworth (then retired and living in France) to replace them, and many graced the gardens until his death in 1979. Ultimately these were also given away, as the process of moving them seasonally to and from the Orangerie was labor intensive.

Today the gardens at Kykuit have evolved, in response both to the interests of the family members who cultivated them over the first ninety years and to the goals and practical requirements of the National Trust for Historic Preservation. The estate today is no longer a private retreat. Of the two hundred and fifty acres within the gates, one-third remains private and two-thirds belong to the National Trust and under the stewardship and administration of the Rockefeller Brothers Fund. The Pocantico Center in the Coach Barn is a venue for conferences and meetings on critical issues related to the Rockefeller Brothers Fund's mission to advance social change that contributes to a more just, sustainable, and peaceful world. It also serves as a community resource and offers public access through a visitation program, lectures, and cultural events.

Yet the words of Bosworth are as evocative today as when they were written in 1919:

> But to know this enchanting hill-top one must experience the early morning with its long shadows and dewy freshness, its fragrance, and the song of birds; or late evening when all is peacefully eloquent of aloofness from the busy world; when the glimmer of the lights of Tarrytown and Nyack far across the Tappan Zee lend a fairylike charm, enhanced now and then by the brilliant searchlights from the river steamboats as they silently move along; or when moonlight caresses the marble statues and makes phosphorescent glint and glitter in the splashing fountains. The impressions left from these and countless similar experiences enrich the memories of those who know the gardens at 'Kijkuit.'[26]

Above and right: In the Inner Garden, Aristide Maillol's Bather Putting Up Her Hair *is silhouetted by the light of the Morning Garden beyond the teahouse. Maillol's* Torso *is juxtaposed with an Etruscan oil jar.*

Opposite: Peter Chinni's Natura Eterna *terminates the principal axis of the Inner Garden.*

Right: Aristide Maillol's Bather Putting Up Her Hair *is flanked by topiaries offering fanciful privacy.*

*Above and right: Sunlight
bouncing off snow highlights
the form and silhouette of the
sculpture.*

Above and left: William Welles Bosworth's design incorporates a series of terraces that allow the formal planting to navigate the steep slope above the Hudson River. Among the original plantings, box-wood hedges have matured into undulating forms interspersed with pines that now stand more than twenty feet tall. A working model of Henry Moore's Nuclear Energy *is juxtaposed with a limestone group of* Hercules and the Nemean Lion *by Orazio Marinali.*

Above: The lowest of the terraces is a putting green, where Gaston Lachaise's Man *is installed.*

Right: Contemporary and classical sculpture turn the Beaux-Arts garden rooms into galleries. Louise Nevelson's Atmosphere and Environment *and Arnaldo Pomodoro's* Traveller's Column *were installed by Nelson Rockefeller; the eighteenth-century limestone groups of* Hercules and the Hydra *and* Hercules and the Nemean Lion *were part of the original Bosworth design.*

Above: A nineteenth-century figure of Amphitrite on the Orange Tree Terrace.

Left: The pavilion on the Swimming Pool Terrace.

*Above: Clipped taxus and
hemlock now stand more than
twenty feet tall.*

Above: Hercules and the
Nemean Lion *amid the hedges
and pines.*

Above and right: Arnaldo Pomodoro's Traveller's Column *holds a corner of the highest terrace. Below, on the putting green, are Aristide Maillol's* Night *(right) and Marino Marini's* Horse.

Above: Max Bill's Triangular Surface *at the entrance to the putting green.*

Left: Alexander Calder's Large Spiny *seems to march across the lawn.*

Above and right: John D. Rockefeller planted the copper beech grove in 1909. A mulitiered and asymmetrical branching structure gives the trees their undulating shape, almost concealing Alexander Liberman's vivid Above II.

Above and left: Granny's Knot *by Shinkichi Tajiri is another inspired art placement in the cooper beech grove, with its interlocking form set against the gnarled tree trunks. The dense planting appeals in all seasons.*

Above and right: The handsomely proportioned Orangerie, designed by William Welles Bosworth in 1908, once housed an extensive collection of orange trees acquired at auction in France. Across the lawn are the greenhouses by Lord & Burnham.

Above and left: Japanese temple lanterns mark the entrance to the tennis lawn from the Brook Garden. Gerhard Marcks's Maja *stands behind them.*

Above: The upturned roof of the Japanese lantern contrasts with the branches of a weeping cherry bending to meet it.

Left: The brilliant winter sun casts strong and intricate shadows on the snow.

Above: The Brook Garden at cherry blossom time.

Right: Magnolias blooming in the Summer Garden.

*Above: Azaleas mark the
entrance to Brook Garden from
the Inner Garden.*

*Right: Dogwoods bloom in the
Brook Garden after the weeping
cherries have flowered.*

Preceding pages: At the southern end of the Inner Garden is a wrought-iron gate leading to the Brook Garden. Reg Butler's attenuated Girl with a Vest *contrasts with Gaston Lachaise's full-figured* Standing Woman.

Above: Dogwoods in the Brook Garden rise high enough to animate the Temple of Aphrodite.

Right: A low boxwood hedge borders the lawn of the forecourt, while a tall hedge beyond encloses the Morning Garden. The urn is one of a pair modeled by Emil Siebein.

Above and right: A monumental staircase leads from the forecourt to a lawn below. Classical elements include a colored-stone mosaic with signs of the Zodiac, urns, and Augustin Pajou's Cupid and Psyche.

Above and opposite: In the Rose Garden, paths radiate out from the fountain to meet a semicircular path at the perimeter. The rubble stone of the Inner Garden walls and teahouse is carried into the pergolas that mark the entrance.

Left and opposite: Abby Aldrich Rockefeller's love of roses is seen here.

Right: George Grey Barnard's Rising Woman *is placed on the lawn below the forecourt.*

Opposite: The swimming pools are paved with black and white pebbles in a classical pattern. In front of the hedge is Spatial Concept: Nature I and II *by Lucio Fontana.*

Above: In a niche on the north facade of the house is Turtle Boy *by Evelyn Longman Batchelder, a student of Daniel Chester French and the first woman elected to the National Academy of Design.*

Opposite: Song of the Vowels *by Jacques Lipchitz is installed on the Orange Tree Terrace above the swimming pools.*

The Japanese Garden at Kykuit

CYNTHIA BRONSON ALTMAN

John D. Rockefeller Jr. and Abby Aldrich Rockefeller were leading collectors of Asian art, initially acquiring sculpture, ceramics, screens, and prints in the early decades of the twentieth century. Their interest deepened as a result of a four-month trip to the Far East—Japan, Korea, and China—in 1921 for the dedication of the Peking Union Medical College, a project initiated by the China Medical Board of the Rockefeller Foundation. The Rockefellers' interest in Asian culture extended to landscape as well, and they established two gardens inspired by the Far East—one, the Japanese Garden at Kykuit and the other at Mount Desert, Seal Harbor, Maine, which gracefully blends eastern and western traditions. The earlier of the two, the Kykuit garden was first created in 1908 and then expanded and altered in the early 1960s.

It is an important example of the Japanese garden in the United States, and its ultimate design combines elements of several types of garden: the stroll garden, the hill and pond, the dry landscape (*kare-sansui*), and the tea garden.

The Japanese Garden was created in the wake of the international expositions of the late nineteenth and early twentieth centuries, which fostered an awareness of the aesthetic traditions of Asia. Japanese villages, temples, and gardens were included in the 1876 Centennial Exposition in Philadelphia, the 1893 World's Columbian Exposition in Chicago, the 1901 Pan-American Exposition in Buffalo, and the 1904 Louisiana Purchase Exposition in St. Louis.

The fascination with the East extended beyond art and design to landscape, encouraged by a new availability of exotic botanical material. Western visitors to Japan in the late 1880s noted a rich gardening culture that supported a large number of commercial nurseries. Western plantsmen became active soon after Japan opened to trade. German botanist Philipp Franz von Siebold established a botanic garden in Nagasaki, with a sale catalogue listing nearly four hundred plants. In 1880 American Louis Boehmer opened Yokohama Nursery for export, promoting the firm with exquisite catalogues of rice paper and precious mica, as used in the most prized of Ukiyo-e-prints. Great varieties of peonies, iris, chrysanthemum, lilies, and wisteria flowed into Europe and North America, where they were planted in Japanese style gardens.[1] Photographs of Isabella Stewart Gardner's 1885 garden in Brookline outside of Boston, one of the earliest private Japanese gardens in this country, show a great a profusion of iris and waterlilies in the still pond. At the Sonnenberg Gardens in Canandaigua in the Finger Lakes region of New York State, a garden and teahouse (very similar to Kykuit's 1909 teahouse) were created between 1906 and 1910 under the direction of K. Wadamori; Takeo Shiota designed a Japanese garden in 1909–10 for Edith and George Gould at Georgian Court, in Lakewood, New Jersey, and in 1915 he planned the garden at Brooklyn Botanic Garden, one of the earliest public Japanese gardens.

Top: Stream in the Japanese Garden.

Above: Japanese lantern by the pool, photographed by Mattie Edwards Hewitt, 1929.

Opposite: The original teahouse, photographed by Mattie Edwards Hewitt, 1929.

Preceding pages: Japanese maples border the path to the dry landscape garden.

The Japanese Garden is to the west of Kykuit, below the formal terraces and somewhat secluded from view from the gardens surrounding the house. The earliest design, by William Welles Bosworth, was a hill and pond garden, gathering the water of the natural wetland area. He and John D. Rockefeller Jr.

> proceeded to plan an artificial Japanese style brook and pond built in a natural depression below the terraces which had always been very wet after rain. The pond would. . . serve several functions: it would beautify the otherwise marshy run-off area; it would serve as a water hazard for the nearby golf course and . . . as a source for dirt fill needed elsewhere, which would defray the cost of building it.[2]

Azaleas, pines, Japanese maple, and weeping cherries were planted. To the north, a path and stream banked with juniper and carefully pruned ornamental shrubs bordered the rolling lawns of the golf course. The fountains and pools in the formal gardens around Kykuit were designed to spill into the stream of the Japanese Garden, which was bordered by daffodils and daylilies, many of which remain today.

The first teahouse was completed in 1909 by the carpenter Uyeda,[3] who had built a model on the Pfizer estate in New Jersey.[4] The panels of outer walls slide into pockets, and shoji move aside to reveal the views of the surrounding gardens. The gardener, Takahashi, first arrived at the gardens in 1910. Specific records from the early years are scarce but indicate that on August 1, 1916, Rockefeller wrote to Bosworth asking him to review the new plant material that Takahashi was ordering. Bosworth reported on the meeting a few days later:

> I stopped at Pocantico on Saturday . . . and interviewed Takahashi—looking at what he has done and wishes to do. It all seems to me to be well advised and advantageous. I recommend supplying him with the additional plants he wants. He thinks the dogs are out of place at the bridge—according to true oriental tradition, and should be built into the bank in some way. I couldn't just make out how. I reminded him of my original scheme of some light bamboo shelters in the open space opposite the tea house.[4]

Top: Stream banked with azaleas.

Above: Lower pond.

Top: Bridge to the teahouse, photographed by Mattie Edwards Hewitt, 1929.

Above: Teahouse pond.

Writing in the privately printed *Gardens of Kijkuit* in 1919, Bosworth pronounced the design a success:

> The waterfalls, miniature mountains, dwarf planting, bridges, lakes and Tea House, built of mahogany, are all according to the best Japanese tradition.

He described the principal elements:

> Weather-beaten rocks, carefully transported from the neighboring woods so that the marks of time should not be obliterated, are here composed in harmonies and contrasts unknown to European art. A variety of stone lanterns ornament these gardens. The watercourse forms a beautiful pond with an island reached by picturesque stepping stones, and after meandering through the hollows along the entrance driveway, tumbles at length into a rocky gorge overshadowed by drooping willow trees.[5]

There were few changes to garden and teahouse in the first half of the twentieth century. In 1960 after the death of John D. Rockefeller Jr., the 1909 mahogany teahouse (today called the Shrine) was moved about five hundred feet west to a grove of white pine. Near this site, an open pond surrounded by maples and weeping cherry today illustrates the character of the first hill and pond garden. Nelson Rockefeller, and his sister-in-law Blanchette Rockefeller commissioned a new teahouse and an elaboration of the garden. She and her husband, John D. Rockefeller 3rd, were deeply engaged with Japan. He first visited in 1929, and in 1953 the couple began to take annual winter trips, often followed by another in the summer; an extended visit with their family in 1955 further cemented their devotion to the arts and culture of Japan. In 1963 they began to form a collection of Asian art, seeking sculpture, screens, ceramics, and prints that are now at Asia Society in New York.

The architect Junzo Yoshimura and the garden designer David Engel were known to the Rockefellers through their collaboration on a structure and garden for the Museum of Modern Art exhibition series "The House in the Garden." After the exhibition closed, Yoshimura's pavilion was given to the City of Philadelphia, and, known as Shofuso or Pine Breeze Villa, still stands in Fairmount Park.

Approaching Yoshimura in November 1960, Mrs. Rockefeller explained that the family sought to redesign the garden "more authentically" and to replace the teahouse with "a very simple and beautiful garden pavilion of a classical style which you know so well along the order of the Katsura Villa garden pavilions."[6]

For Kykuit, Yoshimura designed a small house for the edge of the pond (the house at MoMA was 756 square feet; the Pocantico house is 412). The architectural style, sukiya, dates to the Momoyama era of the sixteenth century. The restrained elegance and traditional rustic simplicity were prized by Japanese nobility, and the style was also used for abbots' quarters within temple precincts. Much of the building was prefabricated in Kyoto by the firm of Nakamura Komuten, and completed on site during the winter of 1961–62.[7]

In the early 1960s, David Engel redesigned and expanded the upper section of the garden. Engel had studied in Kyoto in the 1950s under Tansai Sano, a garden master whose family had tended the dry garden at Ryoan-ji at Daitoku-ji in Kyoto for six generations.

Opposite: Teahouse designed by Junzo Yoshimura, 1961.

At Kykuit, Engel created a two-acre stroll garden through an ever-changing landscape. He described the effect in an essay of August 2013:

> [A] sense of mystery and adventure attends the visitor. Nothing is completely revealed from any single vantage point. Contracting and expanding spaces and contrasts and transitions in mood are created with a variety of path pavings, tiles and stone, edgings, ground covers, trees and shrubs of different textures and hues, walls, fences and screens . . . [T]he garden becomes a series of abstraction, but not copies, of nature . . . a distillation of the essence of the vast world outside, yet subtly revealing the hand of man.[8]

Ancient pines, yew, maples, and cherries remain from the original garden. The new garden was planned around the original pond and course of the stream. The new path begins at the main gate at the edge of the road. Stepping-stones banked by liriope lead over an arched stone bridge through a small gate to a reflecting pond in front of the teahouse. Azaleas border the pond, and to the north, the path divides. One branch leads through a small gate to the dry landscape garden. A meditation garden, the design is patterned on the fifteenth-century garden at the Zen temple Ryoan-ji. Five groups of rocks are arranged within the expanse of raked white gravel. These can be interpreted as islands in a vast sea or mountain peaks rising through banks of clouds or mist. The other branch of the path crosses an arched granite bridge to water-washed rocks and stepping-stones through the middle of a stream and across a deep gorge where carp once swam. The rush of a waterfall twelve feet in height masks all other sound.

An ochre stucco wall capped with dove-brown Kawara roof tiles separates the garden from the open lawns of the golf course to the west. A grove of Golden Grove bamboo shades a section of the upper path. Stones of many shapes and sizes form the pathways: cobblestones from a street in Albany, smooth round river stones, large and small squares of gray granite, and roof tiles placed on edge. Their placement slows one's stride and forces a contemplative pace. A millstone marks the spot where two paths diverge. Stone lanterns, pagodas, and water basins grace the paths.

Opposite, top: Slate shingles turned on end form the path to the teahouse.

Opposite, below: A cascading copper beech and Japanese maples border the dry landscape garden. The raked pattern in the sand suggests movement of water around the stones.

Engel's correspondence relates searching for rocks and boulders for the garden in the pastures and woods to the north:

> Rockery, the vital distinguishing feature of a Japanese garden, was a first consideration in its initial planning . . . With lumber marking crayon in hand, Engel marked with X's a bountiful selection of rocks and boulders, largely from those early stone walls. Those of sculptural quality were destined for evocative groupings; others, with at least one flat face, became stepping stones in paths and stream beds.[8]

In the expanse of gravel to the west of the pond are two conical piles of gravel; a low azalea hedge, clipped to mirror their shape, leads the eye to the rolling lawns and further to distant cliffs across the Hudson. This illustrates the Japanese design principle of *shakkei*, or borrowed scenery, bringing the macrocosm of the outer world into the microcosm of the garden. Dewy mosses and the gray-green lichen cover the walls of stone and lend the soft patina of age— the quality so prized in Japan as *sabi* and *wabi*.

Opposite: A millstone marks the divergence of the paths, one descending the hill to the dry landscape garden and the other following the stream to the pond.

Above and left: Large stones line the watercourse, which spills down to the ponds at the teahouse. The water runs from north to south, bisecting the garden and requiring bridges and stepping-stones that encourage leisurely strolling.

Above: Vivid azaleas contrast with the sober stone of a lantern.

Right: Venerable cherry trees enhance the landscape beside the pond.

Above and left: In spring, azaleas bring rich color to the dense woods.

Overleaf: Stepping-stones rise above a "sea" of gravel. The path to the left leads through an azalea hedge to the garden; the path to the right leads to the pond and the teahouse. Two works by Will Horwitt, Fast Force *(left) and* Sky, *mark the intersection of the paths.*

Above and left: The twisting forms of Japanese maples rise above dense foliage of azalea, boxwood, and a blanket of procumbent juniper.

Overleaf: The teahouse stands in the pond, accessed by a stone bridge. An undulating hedge of clipped azaleas lines the shore, enveloping the tree trunks in its path.

Above and opposite: Sunlight animates the translucent leaves and twisting branches of Japanese maples, creating intricate patterns of light and shadow.

*Above and right: A wall capped
with traditional Japanese tiles
separates the garden from the
golf course. The stone water
basin and bamboo spout
(tsukubai) is a form that has
been used for ritual cleansing
from the period of the earliest
Shinto shrines.*

Above and left: The garden is built into the steep slope above the Hudson River. A narrow set of stone steps leads down to the entrance, but the space is hidden from view until visitors cross the threshold.

Above and right: Large stones bordering the stream and ponds encourage strolling along the edges. Sunlight filtering through the maple canopy reflects color on the surface of the water.

Above and right: The teahouse provides serene views across the pond to the entrance and to the wall and dry landscape garden.

*Above and left: The bark of the
venerable cherry trees around
the pond has a gnarled beauty
of longevity.*

Above and left: Shafts of bamboo sway in the wind, creating a soothing sound. The vivid fall color of the cutleaf Japanese maples at the entrance to the grove contrasts with the green bamboo.

Above and left: Trees and stones are the architectural bones of the garden.

Above: A venerable maple that
was part of the original planting.

Right: A young maple arcs gracefully in front of the spreading
limbs of a much older tree.

Above: South entrance to the dry landscape garden.

Left: Tossed by the wind, the vivid maple leaves seem ablaze.

Above and right: The dry landscape garden is sited at the midpoint of the Japanese Garden, with two entrances from the grove of Japanese maples. To the west, the limbs of a monumental copper beech form a green "curtain" above the wall.

*Above, left, and overleaf:
Through the seasons, the dry
garden itself is unchanged, but its
atmosphere responds to changes
in the light and the landscape
around it.*

Above and left: The 1909 tea-house, now known as the Shrine, in late fall and in winter.

Abby Aldrich Rockefeller Garden

TODD FORREST AND CASSIE BANNING

The first element that visitors to the Abby Aldrich Rockefeller Garden see is not its pale-pink, tile-capped Chinese wall, which emerges unexpectedly at the end of a path through the Maine woods, nor is it the sweep of the pagoda roof of the South Gate through which they are invited to enter. It is a moss verge that lines the path to the garden. While it appears completely natural, this luxurious green carpet has been carefully cultivated.

This subtle device is a fitting introduction to a garden that combines sophisticated design and meticulous horticulture within a splendid natural setting. In 1926 John D. Rockefeller Jr. and Abby Aldrich Rockefeller retained celebrated landscape gardener Beatrix Farrand to design a garden for The Eyrie, their summer cottage on the flanks of Barr Hill in Seal Harbor on Mount Desert Island in Maine.

The garden the Rockefellers envisioned was unlike anything Farrand had designed in the past. It would be influenced by gardens the Rockefellers had seen during their travels to Asia, serve as a setting for their growing collection of Asian sculpture, and provide an ample supply of cut flowers.

Farrand's design realized the Rockefellers' expansive vision. She created a sequence of spaces that gracefully integrate Asian and European garden styles in an interplay between native and ornamental, in the form of a naturalistic woodland sculpture garden and a formal flower garden. The brilliance of her design is revealed immediately upon stepping through the enclosing wall at the South Gate and venturing onto the Spirit Path, a linear garden laid out according to the principles of traditional Chinese Imperial tomb design. Six pairs of stone tomb figures from Korea, representing civil and military officials, flank a gravel path set within plantings of low-growing native plants including mosses, bunchberry, lowbush blueberry, and ferns. The path ends in a small clearing in the woods with views of Little Long Pond and the surrounding mountains.

Only a short walk from the Spirit Path, the adjacent flower garden is horticulturally a world apart. Once the site of a vast cutting garden created by Farrand and Mrs. Rockefeller to provide flowers for rooms of The Eyrie, the flower garden is as strongly influenced by Gertrude Jekyll and classic English border design as the Spirit Path is by the cultural landscapes of China.

As Farrand wrote in her notes, "As flower gardens in the occidental sense of the word are unknown in China and Korea, it was clearly necessary to disassociate the figures from the actual flowers and to keep them as guardians of the entrance walk and surrounded by naturalistic and inconspicuous plantings."

A moss-covered flagstone walk leads from the Spirit Path, through the vase-shaped Bottle Gate, and into the Oval Garden (also known as the Green Garden) beyond. The Oval Garden features a lawn with a small rectangular reflecting pool surrounded by a calming mix of shade-tolerant perennials and shrubs in shades of green, lavender, white, or silver. Shaded benches offer views northward to the iconic Moon Gate, a circular opening in the Chinese wall that links the garden to

Top: Bottle Gate.

Above: Spirit Path.

Preceding pages: View from the Frog Pond across the Spirit Path to the annual garden. A fourteenth/fifteenth-century Korean lantern is set in the moss surrounding the pond.

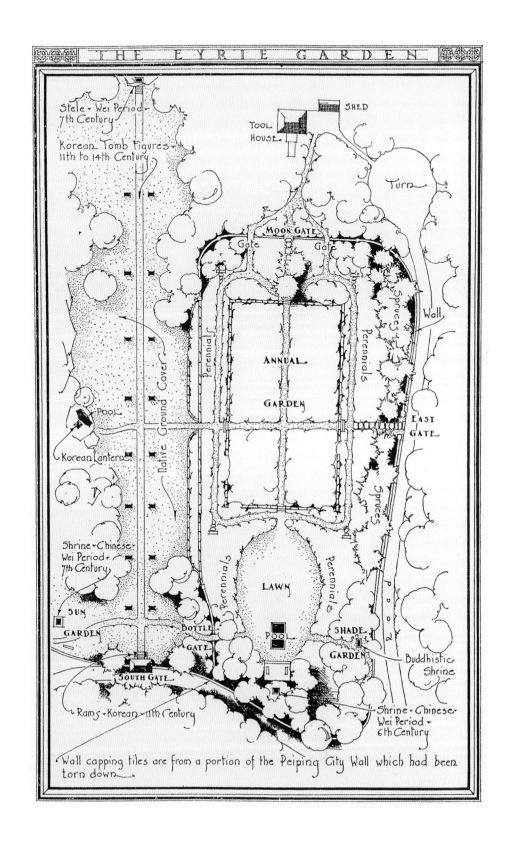

Right: Original plan of the garden by Beatrix Farrand.

the surrounding forest. Between the Oval Garden and the Moon Gate are profusely planted flower beds and borders arranged around a sunken rectangular lawn.

The influence of English planting design can be seen most clearly in the borders that step up from the sunken lawn. The west side of the garden is planted with flowers in colors on the warm side of the spectrum, while cooler pastels predominate in the eastern borders. Some annuals and perennials, including white daisies, blue ageratums, and plants with silver foliage, are repeated throughout the borders to unify the composition.

Much of the color in the borders comes from masses of annuals that represent about 60 percent of the plantings. Gardeners grow the majority of these annuals from seed, which they start in greenhouses in early spring. Some hard-to-find heirloom varieties of heliotrope, scented geranium, and marguerite daisy are grown from cuttings taken each year from stock plants. Dahlias, an important source of late-season color, are lifted each fall, overwintered in a cellar, potted up in April, and planted in the borders for August flowering.

The extravagant color provided by the annuals throughout the growing season allows the horticulturists to include a range of perennials and shrubs even though they may flower for a only a week or two. Daylilies are featured, as are hydrangeas such as 'Blue Billow' and 'Blue Boy'. Tall perennials—delphinium, 'Lemon Queen' sunflower, hollyhock, globe thistle, plume poppy, and giant meadowsweet—provide scale in the backs of the borders.

While an uninterrupted display of color has always been the top priority of the garden's stewards, fragrance is also an important consideration in the design of the borders. Many fragrant plants, including heliotrope, nemesia, lilies, lavender, garden phlox, and hosta, have been included since Farrand and Mrs. Rockefeller developed the first planting lists. The perfume of trumpet lily hybrids is a highlight from mid-July through mid-August.

Gardeners work throughout the year to ensure that the garden will be radiant in the height of summer. Winter is filled with ordering seed, recordkeeping, and

Opposite: The garden is a magical combination of Asian, European, and American elements set within a clearing in the Maine woods.

searching for new plants for the following year. Plant propagation takes precedence in early spring when the garden is emerging from its winter dormancy. As the weather warms, gardeners gently remove leaves that have accumulated on the moss over the winter—an essential step in the cultivation of the lush carpets of moss.

Spring is slow to come to Mount Desert—it is not uncommon to have snow linger until April. The planting season begins in earnest at the end of May and continues throughout June. Cold-tolerant annuals such as snapdragons, dusty miller, and marguerite daisies and new perennials are planted first. Heliotrope, salvia, verbena, and zinnia, which need relatively warm nights to thrive, are planted last.

Summer is the high season for visitors and plants alike. During the warmer months, gardeners are fully occupied with deadheading, staking, watering, raking the gravel paths, and the countless other detailed tasks that give the Abby Aldrich Rockefeller Garden its reputation for horticultural excellence. Managing a rogue's gallery of familiar garden maladies (slugs, snails, Japanese beetles, red lily beetle, and powdery mildew, to name a few) demands considerable attention in summer, and gardeners are always on the lookout for new foes.

Fall brings fewer human visitors, but is an important season for bees, butterflies, and migrating hummingbirds. The horticultural work shifts to preparing for the long Maine winter. Annuals are removed as their flowers fade and used to make compost that will be added back to the garden in future years. After the first hard frost, the dahlias are dug and perennials cut back. When the ground freezes, spruce boughs harvested from the surrounding forest are laid over the delphinium, lilies, lavender, and tender perennials. Gravel is removed from the paths and stored for the winter to keep it clean and protect the moss verges from contamination during snowplowing season.

Created through a collaboration between a talented designer and discerning clients and thoughtfully nurtured for ninety years, the Abby Aldrich Rockefeller Garden defies easy characterization. It is a formal garden, a naturalistic garden, an intimate garden, an expansive garden, a sculpture garden, a flower garden, an Asian garden, a Maine garden, a historic garden, and a garden of constant change. Above all else, it is a gardener's garden full of surprising details and brimming with expertly tended plants.

Opposite: The garden is carefully planned and planted to come into peak bloom at the height of the summer season.

Above, right, and overleaf: A Korean lantern marks
the entrance to the garden, which is enclosed by an
undulating pink-stucco wall capped with tiles acquired
by the Rockefellers in Beijing.

*Above: Seated Buddha
Shakyamuni at the Moon Gate.*

*Right: The South Gate is
the principal entrance to the
garden. Mythical creatures dec-
orate the traditional Chinese
pagoda roof.*

Above: Detail of roof tiles at the South Gate.

Left: A pair of fourteenth/ fifteenth-century granite rams flank the entrance from the South Gate.

Above and right: Lining the Spirit Path are fourteenth/fifteenth-century Korean tomb figures. A Chinese Buddhist votive stele terminates the path.

Right: Elaborately carved armor, a helmet, and a sword identify this figure as a military official.

Left: The deep greens of the pines and moss set off the weathered surface of the figure and the surrounding stones.

Overleaf: Sculptures are set in the woods off the Spirit Path.

*Above and right: A small stone
frog gives the pond above the
Spirit Path its name.*

Above: Moss and pine needles carpet the forest floor adjacent to the Spirit Path.

Left: The Spirit Path terminates in a circular clearing with a Chinese Buddhist votive stele at the center. Octagonal Korean pillars flank the entrance.

Above: A fifth/sixth-century Chinese pagoda overlooks a lily pool set into the lawn at the south end of the garden.

Right: Granite steps ascend to a seventeenth-century gilt-bronze Chinese seated Buddha Amitabha.

Above and left: The South Gate and the Bottle Gate.

*Above and left: Seated Buddha
Shakyamuni outside the Moon
Gate is mounted on a lotus
pedestal.*

Above and left: Views through the Moon Gate to the Buddha Shakamuni and looking back into the garden from the path. A pair of Korean granite animals guard the entrance, which is framed by towering ostrich ferns.

Overleaf: Originally planned as a cutting garden, the central lawn gives the eye a place to rest amid the polychromatic tumult of the flower beds.

Above: A mass of magenta Astilbe 'Superba' seems to float above the central lawn.

Left: Spires of blue delphinium provide a pleasing contrast with the "hot" colors that predominate in the borders on the east side of the flower garden.

Above: Masses of petunia, ageratum, and flowering tobacco add midsummer flash and fragrance to the flower garden.

Right: Cooler colors prevail in the borders on the west side of the central lawn.

Above: Snapdragons and garden phlox are old-fashioned favorites that have been cultivated in the garden since Abby Aldrich Rockefeller's day, while lilies are a more recent addition.

Left: Perfectly raked gravel paths draw visitors through the flower borders.

Above and right: Plant height increases from the path edge to the back of the borders, creating a cascade of color from back to front. Expertly staked lilies and delphiniums rise above masses of low annuals.

Above: A cheerful vignette featuring petunias, snapdragons, ageratums, sneezeweeds, and phlox.

Above: The spiky heads of globe thistle contrast with the soft flowers of sneezeweed and ageratum.

Above: By midsummer, the granite stonework throughout the garden is almost entirely concealed by lush new growth.

Left: The flower garden is as bright and colorful as the adjacent woods are dark and mossy.

Above: The large leaves of flow-ering tobacco provide welcome texture in the border.

Opposite: A vigorous clump of black-eyed Susan with hundreds of bright yellow flowers.

Above: A variety of low-growing dahlias brighten the garden from late summer until autumn's first frost.

Left: Tall plants such as plume poppy and perennial sunflower add scale to the back of the border.

Above: The addition of freshly cut flowers to a stone basin is a small, yet powerful gesture.

Right: Scented geranium and lamb's ear grace the edges of a gravel path at the north end of the flower garden.

Overleaf: View through the East Gate into the garden.

EXPERIENCING AND PHOTOGRAPHING THE ROCKEFELLER FAMILY GARDENS

Larry Lederman

It rained on my first visit to Kykuit, heavily enough to coat the leaves and trunks of the stand of beech trees I had come to photograph. I had a slicker, but I couldn't work in the downpour. To wait it out I sat at the base of one of the large beeches with an massive trunk, sheltered under its huge canopy. From that vantage point, I looked around.

There were contemporary sculptures sitting in the midst of the trees. A surprise. Ordinarily, sculpture is set in an open space and given pride of place. Here the placement was intended to adorn the grove. The one near me, an Alexander Liberman, recognizable from its stacked, bright-red cylinders, was large, but it appeared comparatively small in this wood. Indeed, the bulky cylinders seemed to take the shape of an animal, some creature out of its element, running among the elephantine beeches to seek shelter in the wood, much like a deer.

 On my left, as I shimmied along the base of the tree to stay out of the rain and get a better view, was an eggshell-colored sculpture called *Granny's Knot*, as twisted as the beech limbs turning to the light. A mind was at work. Later, when I could move about, I found the emerald golf course, and, beyond, vistas of the Hudson looking to the horizon. This is an immense estate, of course, meant to be grand, but I readily concluded on my first visit in August 2011, that the gardens were multilayered, intended to give pleasure.

There was much to discover, based on a rich history, laid down at the outset in 1909 by John D. Rockefeller and then his son John Jr., followed by Nelson A. Rockefeller. In the beech grove, I had come across a few of Nelson's embellishments, some touches of whimsy. Placing his sculpture collection was a serious undertaking for him, and he took pains to integrate it into the gardens, softening the formal areas, rendering some grand garden rooms into intimate galleries.

I was to learn that each generation had significantly expressed itself and changed Kykuit, as Cynthia Bronson Altman authoritatively describes in her essay. For a garden with this longevity, change is inevitable. Indeed, gardens by their very nature are impermanent, although venerable gardens give the illusion of immutability. Without care, they decline rapidly and the remnants lose their character. The Japanese Garden suffered from neglect for a time, until Nelson Rockefeller made it his own. Even if some gardens are meant to be a monument to their maker, that intention is not enough to sustain them. As Robert Pogue Harrison in his book *Gardens* has observed: "Few defy the ravages of time. If anything they exist to re-enchant the present." And that can only happen because they are joyous and others want to experience them.

The Rockefeller family gardens are diverse. And each has its own character. In this grouping, I include the Abby Aldrich Rockefeller Garden in Maine. It is the family's summer garden, a walled Asian-style garden in the midst of the Maine woods, which has an unexpected richness and originality, intended to complement the family's garden experience at Kykuit and provide a refuge.

This was the family garden I visited first, before ever seeing Kykuit. The enclosing wall is pink stucco topped with ochre ceramic tiles from Beijing. These were not tiles for the American market or copies. The Rockefellers salvaged them from a demolished wall in the old city, and had them shipped to Maine. And from 1926 to 1930 Mrs. Rockefeller worked with Beatrix Farrand on the garden. Neither had any experience with oriental gardens. Farrand was an accomplished garden designer, but she had not visited Asia. The garden is a joint work of imagination. As such it violates all the rules. It is green and cerebral and serene at its entrance and on a first stroll of its paths, but it breaks away from its contemplative Asian origins. In the center, its core, it is hot and emotional, filled with a flower garden that dazzles with color from annuals and perennials chosen to come to peak in August while the family resides in Maine. The experience of the garden in Maine led me to seek out the family garden at Kykuit.

And I found what I regard as its counterpart at Kykuit, the Japanese stroll garden designed and built in 1909. While the Kykuit estate gardens are expansive with vistas that look out over the Palisades, offering remarkable views and stunning sunsets, the Japanese Garden is walled and self-contained, a garden full of diversions and enchantments.

It was originally designed as a replica of a garden in Kyoto, but it had become overgrown and neglected by the time Nelson Rockefeller moved into Kykuit. He brought it back and enhanced it, working with a Japanese architect and an American landscape designer. Cynthia Altman discusses the important changes thoughtfully made, which significantly improved the garden and its pleasures. With each change, great pains were taken to be authentic. Longevity, however, adds its own patina and character, which makes the Japanese Garden an extraordinary place all its own.

The sense of serenity is ever present in the Japanese Garden, enhanced by its fine design and a contemplative dry sand garden, regularly raked, with complex stones and a bench that draws you away from the quotidian. It is also stunningly beautiful, and surprisingly hot at its core in the spring and the fall. In the spring, bountiful azaleas are filled with dazzling flowers in hot pinks, rich reds, and blinding whites that are transporting; in the fall the venerable cutleaf maples turn scarlet and then an orange deeper than the Beijing tiles in Maine, colors so arresting that they are hard to believe. The garden is layered on the side of a hill facing west and the afternoon light sets the maples on fire and the autumn winds blow the sharp-edged cut leaves so that the sparks appear to fly upward.

Good gardens are sited for the light, which the trees and plantings affect and make singular over time. Kykuit also benefits from the Hudson and is a microclimate with its own temperature. You can say that it has its own light. The Maine garden is a clearing in an old-growth forest, giving a sense of ancient light. The particular experience in each of such light is one of the pleasures of being in a good garden.

My task as a photographer, and one of my pleasures, was to get to know the gardens and to experience the ranges of their light over a number of years, and then to anticipate the changes in order to capture them. Each of the photographs finds the expression of the light on the gardens; and each is of an ephemeral moment that offers sparkling facets. All the photographs, taken together, present the immediacy of the experience of place, while creating, as only photographs can, a sense of immersion in the gardens, unbounded by their formalities, and an indelible record of them.

This book is the product of a long-term commitment and of love for the gardens. And in this book, I am pleased to be able to present the photographs to you for what they are and to share them all with you.

NOTES

THE FORMAL GARDENS AT KYKUIT

1 Much of this land is open to the public today. Kykuit is a property of the National Trust for Historic Preservation and open for tours. To the north, the fields and farm buildings became the Stone Barns Center for Food and Agriculture in 2004. To the west and further north, The Rockefeller State Park Preserve maintains woodlands and many of the fifty-five miles of carriage roads laid out in the early twentieth century.

2 Time at Pocantico was spent in the managing the property and focusing on philanthropies, including the University of Chicago, The Rockefeller Institute for Medical Research (1901), the General Education Board (1902), the Rockefeller Foundation (1913).

3 Warren Manning also worked at Forest Hill, John D. Rockefeller's residence in Cleveland, Ohio.

4 John D. Rockefeller, *Random Reminiscences of Men and Events, 1908* (Tarrytown, NY: Sleepy Hollow Press, 1983) 34–37.

5. Rockefeller, *Random Reminiscences.*

6 Robert H. Moulton, "Wonderful Gardens at Pocantico Hills," *International Studio*, November 1919: xix.

7 The architects were Delano & Aldrich; Ogden Codman designed the interiors. The house was altered in 1913, and the facade today reflects the classical influence of Bosworth.

8 Platt's text originally appeared as two articles in *Harper's New Monthly Magazine* in the summer of 1893. Platt designed Villa Turicum in Lake Forest, Illinois, for Rockefeller's daughter Edith and her husband, Harold McCormick in 1908–18. The lakefront terraces reflect those of the Villa d'Este and the entrance front is based on Villa Mondragone at Frascati.

9 The Borghese vase was made in the first century B.C.E. for a Roman garden, and is now in the Louvre. Replicas are in the gardens of Versailles and other European and English gardens. The Warwick vase was found at Hadrian's Villa in Tivoli in 1771 by Gavin Hamilton and sent to Scotland, where it is now in the Burrell Collection in Glasgow.

10 William Welles Bosworth, "The Gardens at Pocantico Hills, Estate of John D. Rockefeller, Esq.," *The American Architect*, January 4, 1911, vol. XLIX, no. 1828: 34.

11 Francine du Plessix Gray, "Anatomy of a Collector: Nelson Rockefeller," *Art in America* (April 1965): 27.

12 Nelson A. Rockefeller, Westchester Arts Council talk, 1977, SUNY Purchase, transcript at the Rockefeller Archive Center.

13 In 1911, the original figure of Oceanus was moved to the Bargello for protection from the elements. Romanelli carved the replica in the Boboli Garden today as well as the version at Kykuit.

14 *The Gardens of Kijkuit*, privately printed, 1919, unpaginated, photographs by Arnold Genthe, and text by Bosworth, edited and approved by John D. Rockefeller Jr. In 1917 after consulting with the gardener, Bosworth recommended first a row of white candy tuft and then a center of yellow. The gardener thought portulaca would be the best, due to the difficulty with pansies and snapdragons. Rockefeller Archive Center, RGIII 21, homes, box 17 folder 170.

15 Platt also used this pavilion as a model for structures in his gardens at Faulkner Farm (1896) and The Weld (1901), both in Brookline, Massachusetts.

16 Bosworth, "The Gardens at Pocantico Hills": 8.

17 William Welles Bosworth, *The Altoviti Aphrodite*, 1920. The sculpture was discovered in the garden of the Altoviti family in Florence.

18 *The Gardens of Kijkuit.*

19 *The Gardens of Kijkuit.*

20 Shurcliff's planting plan is at the Rockefeller Archive Center.

21 *The Gardens of Kijkuit.*

22 Rockefeller Archive Center, Letterbooks 122/357; 133/272, 158/490; from F.W. Smythe, New York, 1909 and Henry A. Dreer, Philadelphia, 1910.

23 The original was once thought to be by Donatello but today is attributed to the circle of Antonio Rossellino (1427/28–1479) and Benedetto da Maiano (1441?–1497), commissioned by Cosimo il Vecchio de' Medici (1389–1464) and Piero de Cosimo de'Medici (1416–1469).

24 By Frederick C. Roth, 1919, commissioned for the gardens.

25. Unpublished research, March 2008. Claudia Leslie corresponded with the current owners, now called Château de Villaines in Louplande. The popular press a few years later, apparently having interviewed Smythe, reports an auction with spirited bidding between "the New Yorker and a very animated and ultimately disappointed Frenchman" said to represent the house of Rothschild.

26 *The Gardens of Kijkuit.*

THE JAPANESE GARDENS
AT KYKUIT

1 "The Golden Age of Japanese Export Nurseries, 1880–1930," exhibition at the Linley Library of the Royal Horticultural Society, London, 2016.

2 Albert I Berger., *My Father's House at Pocantico Hills: Kykuit and the Business Education of John D. Rockefeller Jr.,*1985, 221. Unpublished manuscript at the Rockefeller Archive Center.

3 Only surnames are recorded for both Uyeda and Takahashi, and research on each is continuing.

4 Hugh J. McCauley, AIA, *National Historic Landmark Survey and Historic Structures Report of John D. Rockefeller's Estate at Pocantico Hills, Westchester County, New York*, 1994, 206.

5 *The Gardens of Kijkuit.*

6 Nelson A. Rockefeller possessions, Rockefeller Archive Center, box 24.

7 On December 8, 1962, a Ridgepole Ceremony was held, with Shinto, Buddhist, and Christian prayers for the protection of the house from all the elements, and for prosperity and safety for the craftsmen, engineers, architects, and owners.

8 David Engel, *The Japanese Garden*, unpublished essay sent from Dhiang Mai, Thailand, August, 2013.

9 Engel, *The Japanese Garden.*

ACKNOWLEDGMENTS

My deep thanks to:

Elizabeth White of The Monacelli Press for her abiding interest in the book and brilliant editorial direction.

John Maggiotto for his invaluable help in reviewing and preparing in the images for printing.

My brother, Ed Lederman, fellow photographer and companion on many of my photographic travels.

Kitty Hawks, my wife, whose keen eye and judgment guided the project from the beginning.

—Larry Lederman

ILLUSTRATION CREDITS

The American Architect, July 1911 18 top

Avery Architectural and Fine Arts Library, Columbia University 33, 88

Environmental Design Archives, Beatrix Farrand Collection, University of California, Berkeley 141

The Gardens of Kykuit 18 below

Kykuit, National Trust for Historic Preservation 21 below

Library of Congress 19

Maxfeld Parrish Family LLC/Vaga 22 top

New-York Historical Society 24, 34, 88, 89

Rockefeller Archive Center 18 below, 20, 21 top, 22 below, 23, 38